GW00498987

Asian Vegetables

CHINESE STYLE COOKING

by
Carrie C. Brown
photographed by
Allan J. Dougherty

Jain Publishing Company
Fremont, California

Library of Congress Cataloging-in-Publication Data

Brown, Carrie C. (Carrie Chu), 1938-
    Asian vegetables / by Carrie C. Brown ;
  photographed by Allan J. Dougherty.
        p.   cm.
    ISBN 0-87573-031-0
    1. Cookery (Vegetables) 2. Cookery, Chinese.
  I. Dougherty, Allan J. II. Title.
  TX801.B74 1994
  641.6'5—dc20   93-33445
                                            CIP

Printed in Hong Kong

In memory of my father,
Shiu Cheung Chu

INTRODUCTION

Bok choy! Daikon! Jicama! Kabocha!
    Interesting-looking vegetables with exotic names tantalize the curious cook. Suddenly, they seem to be everywhere. You might find some in the main aisle of the produce section of a big supermarket, or you might happen on some hidden in a corner in a tiny neighborhood store. Many of the names have no English translation, as if you are expected to be perfectly knowledgeable about them. Clearly, the uninitiated cook is faced with a problem. How to fix them? Is there a right way and a wrong way?
    This book is a starting point. It covers ten vegetables that are commonly used in Chinese cooking. Some, such as chiles and kabocha squash, are native to South America but have been adopted, hybridized, and incorporated into the Chinese cuisine. Most of the leafy greens originated in Asia and came to the West with the Chinese immigrants many years ago. Until recently, they have been largely overlooked and hard to find. Now they show up in supermarkets everywhere. They await your discovery. This book is a buying guide and can accompany you to supermarkets, Oriental stores, or farmers' markets.
    The names of the vegetables are often bewildering; different varieties often have names that sound quite a bit alike. Whenever possible, the labels under which they are

sold in supermarkets are the primary names used in this book. Variations and aliases are also listed.

Each of the ten vegetables has its own unique texture, taste, color, and smell. These are discussed in detail at the beginning of each section. The accompanying recipes are basic and simple; they were chosen because they emphasize the dominant characteristics of the vegetables. Also, they are vegetarian, using no meat or seafood.

More than other peoples of the world, the Chinese understand and respect their vegetables. Foods such as Chinese cabbage and mustard greens are the mainstay of the everyday diet, and over time many cooking methods were developed to make them interesting. This book describes the ways to enhance the flavors of the mild vegetables and tame the pungency of the strong-tasting ones. You may notice that the vegetables are seldom eaten raw as salads. The most delicate ones are usually briefly cooked, parboiled or stir-fried so that the raw taste is removed but all the freshness is retained. Steaming, simmering, or braising is often used for tougher or strong-tasting vegetables. Mixed vegetable dishes are commonly prepared by first parboiling or briefly stir-frying each ingredient individually. Slow, gentle cooking then tenderizes and unifies the flavors. The results are often surprising and varied.

Vegetables do not have to be boring! Let this book introduce you to some eating experiences that are new, exciting, and nutritious.

BASIC STAPLES AND CONDIMENTS

The following are the main staples and condiments mentioned in this book. They are basic to Chinese cooking and are generally inexpensive. Increasingly, major supermarkets are stocking them. Oriental markets offer better selection and prices.

Bean Threads Made from mung beans, these noodles are also known as Saifun, cellophane noodles, and shiny noodles. They look like nylon fishing line and should be softened in cold water before cooking. Overcooking turns them into a slippery mess.

Black Beans, fermented Salt-preserved and fermented black soybeans are very pungent. They should be rinsed before using, then mashed with a little sugar and oil to temper their flavor. A bottled paste, additionally flavored with garlic and sugar, is readily available.

Coriander Leaves Known also as Chinese parsley or cilantro, this herb's strong aroma is an acquired taste. Store the fresh sprigs, like cut flowers, in a tall glass, with the stems just touching the water; cover the leaves with a plastic bag, and put the glass in the refrigerator. Ground coriander is not a substitute.

Five Spice Powder A mixture of Chinese star anise, cinnamon, fennel, Szechwan peppers and cloves, this powder is commonly associated with Chinese roast duck and pork. Used in vegetarian dishes, its robust aroma imparts a meaty flavor.

Ginger Fresh ginger is definitely the most commonly used seasoning in Chinese cooking. It gives a fresh, sharp aroma to food and is especially good for neutralizing fishy and strong meat odors. Choose a plump piece with a smooth, shiny skin, and store it in a paper (not plastic) bag in the refrigerator.

Mushrooms, dried Black mushrooms, when dried, take on a chewy texture and intense flavor. The best variety is about 1 ½ inches in diameter, thick, and meaty. Before using, soak the mushrooms in water for 15 to 20 minutes and remove the stems. The soaking water can be strained and used in sauces and soups.

Rice Chinese, as well as Southeast Asians and Indians, prefer long-grain white rice. Aromatic varieties are becoming increasingly available. These include Delta Rose and Texmati grown in the United States, Basmati from India, and Jasmine from Thailand. Short-grain rice tends to be stickier and is used in Japanese cooking. Instant and parboiled rice have a "processed" taste and should be avoided.

Rice Noodles Dried rice noodles look like brittle nylon fishing line. The most popular variety is somewhat thinner than spaghetti and is available in most supermarkets. It comes in packages under a variety of names: Rice Sticks, Maifun, and Bihon.

Sesame Oil Chinese sesame oil, as compared to the lighter Middle Eastern variety, is dark and distinctively fragrant. It is used sparingly and is often sprinkled on food just before dishing up.

Soy Sauce A discriminating cook uses at least two varieties: thin soy sauce is light and delicate, and is used in dishes where the original colors of the ingredients are to be preserved (for example, fried rice and egg dishes); thick soy sauce is darker and sweeter, and is used to give body and color to braised dishes and stews. There are other interesting variations: "lite" soy sauce is lower in sodium, but does not taste authentic; "teriyaki" sauce has sugar, garlic and other seasonings added, and is handy as a dipping sauce or marinade.

Tofu Fresh bean curd cakes come in two basic forms, firm and soft, which often are mistakenly called Chinese and Japanese, respectively. Both are very perishable and should be kept for no more than three or four days. Discoloration and a bad smell indicate spoilage. Bean curd cutlets are cakes that have most of the water removed; some are further seasoned with soy sauce and spices and have a smoky flavor. Firm and chewy, they are widely used as meat substitutes and are a good source of protein.

Turnip, pickled Dried and preserved in salt and ground chile, pickled turnip adds zest to soups and stir-fried dishes. It can be kept indefinitely in a covered jar in the refrigerator.

Vegetarian Oyster Sauce Distilled from mushrooms, this imitation of the famous Cantonese sauce imparts the same velvety texture and wild aroma to everything it touches. It keeps for a long time in the refrigerator.

E asily available and inexpensive, a bunch of bok choy can be from 10 to 15 inches high, depending on the season and the maturity of the plant. It is most abundant in the winter months. The thick white stalks are succulent and crunchy; the dark green leaves are slightly peppery, becoming mellow and sweet when cooked.

To prepare bok choy, separate the stalks and wash well. Cut the ribs diagonally into ½-inch slices and the leaves into 1-inch pieces. Bok choy tends to exude a lot of water during cooking and is excellent in soups and stews. Stir-frying should be done very briskly over high heat, with enough oil to seal the pieces and to avoid excessive loss of water.

Baby bok choy is not just a young version of the vegetable but rather a different variety. It consists of small, pale green heads of tender stalks and leaves, which are best left whole or split lengthwise. Very mild and sweet, it must be handled with great care during stir-frying, steaming, or boiling, because overcooking makes it stringy.

Bok Choy Chinese White Cabbage
Baby Bok Choy, Xiao Baicai

Baby Bok Choy, Home-style

4 bunches baby bok choy
1 tablespoon oil
3 slices fresh ginger, peeled
2 cloves garlic, pressed
1 tablespoon dry sherry
2 tablespoons water
1 teaspoon sesame oil
Salt, to taste
Sauce:
    1 teaspoon cornstarch
    3 tablespoons water
    ½ teaspoon sugar
    ½ teaspoon thin soy sauce

1. Trim off the tough outer leaves and root ends of the bok choy. The young, tender hearts should be about 6 inches long. Split them lengthwise. Wash carefully.

2. Mix the sauce ingredients in a bowl.

3. In a large frying pan, heat 1 tablespoon of oil. Add the ginger and garlic and stir-fry briskly. One by one, carefully turn the bok choy hearts in the oil.

4. Add 1 tablespoon of dry sherry and 2 tablespoons of water. Cover the pan and cook until the bok choy turns a bright green, about 2 minutes.

5. Uncover and push the bok choy to the side of the pan. Stir the sauce mixture and add to the pan. When the sauce thickens, stir in 1 teaspoon of sesame oil. Correct seasoning with salt.

6. Turn the bok choy in the sauce to coat evenly. Serve immediately.

Braised Mixed Vegetables

6 medium-size dried mushrooms
8 ounces bok choy
2 ounces sugar peas, trimmed
4 ounces jicama, peeled
1 small carrot, peeled
4 tablespoons oil
1 ounce bean threads
2 slices ginger, peeled
1 tablespoon vegetarian oyster sauce
Salt and pepper, to taste

1. Soak the dried mushrooms in water until they are soft. Discard the stems. Drain the caps, reserving the soaking water.

2. Cut the bok choy crosswise into 1-inch pieces and the jicama and carrot into 1 x 2-inch slices.

3. Heat the oil in a heavy pot. With scissors, cut the bean threads into 3-inch lengths. Deep-fry them by the handful;

they should puff up immediately. Remove and put aside.

4. Drain most of the oil, leaving about 1 tablespoon in the pot. In separate batches, stir-fry the sugar peas, bok choy, carrot, mushrooms, and jicama, adding a little oil to the pot between vegetables.

5. Lastly, add some oil to the pan and stir-fry the ginger. Return everything except the sugar peas to the pot. Add ½ cup of the reserved soaking water, cook gently for 15 minutes. Add the sugar peas. Season with oyster sauce, salt, and pepper. Serve immediately.

Crunchy and slightly bitter, Chinese broccoli has a stronger flavor than its cousin, the western broccoli. The stems are thinner, the leaves more tender, and the flower heads much smaller. Chinese broccoli is at its best in the winter months, when a touch of frost intensifies its flavor.

To prepare Chinese broccoli, pull off and discard the larger leaves, exposing the inner stalks and their tender leaves. Take each head and gently bend it. It will snap at the point where tenderness begins. Cut the stalks into 3-inch lengths, or leave them whole. Save the thicker stems and tough leaves for making stock.

Chinese broccoli can be steamed or boiled and then dressed with oil and soy sauce. Stir-frying brings out its best qualities, and splashing it with sherry and a small amount of sugar seems to tame its pungency while enhancing its crunchiness.

The recipes for Chinese broccoli can be used equally well with western broccoli.

Chinese Broccoli
Gai Lan, Jielan, Chinese Kale

Crunchy Chinese Broccoli

8 ounces Chinese broccoli, trimmed
2 cups water
½ teaspoon salt
3 tablespoons oil
1 clove garlic, crushed
1 green onion, chopped
2 slices ginger, peeled
2 tablespoons vegetarian oyster sauce

1. Trim and clean the Chinese broccoli, using only the tender stalks. Leave them whole.

2. Bring 2 cups of water to a boil along with the salt and 1 tablespoon of oil. Parboil the broccoli, removing it as soon as it turns a bright green, about 1 minute. Drain and cool immediately in cold running water. Drain again and set aside.

3. In a small frying pan, heat 2 tablespoons of oil. Add the garlic, chopped green onion, and ginger. Return the broccoli to the pan and toss lightly. As soon as the broccoli is coated with the aromatic oil, remove it to a serving plate.

4. Drizzle the oyster sauce over the broccoli. Serve immediately.

Chinese Broccoli and Bean Curd

12 ounces Chinese broccoli, trimmed
6 ounces smoked bean curd
2 tablespoons oil
2 slices ginger, peeled, minced
2 cloves garlic, minced
1 tablespoon water
½ teaspoon salt
½ teaspoon sugar
1 teaspoon cornstarch
2 tablespoons water
½ teaspoon sesame oil
Marinade:
    2 teaspoons thick soy sauce
    2 teaspoons dry sherry
    1 teaspoon sugar
    ¼ teaspoon five-spice powder

1. Cut the trimmed broccoli into 2-inch lengths.

2. Mix the marinade ingredients in a bowl. Cut the bean curd into ¼-inch slices. Marinate them for 15 minutes.

3. Heat 1 tablespoon of oil in a frying pan. Add the ginger and garlic, and then the broccoli. Stir-fry them briskly, about 1 minute. Add 1 tablespoon of water. Cover the pan and cook the broccoli for 1 to 2 minutes, keeping it crunchy. Add the salt and sugar. Remove and keep warm.

4. Add 1 tablespoon of oil to the pan. Drain the bean curd slices, reserving the marinade. Brown them on both sides.

5. Add the marinade and the broccoli to the pan and toss briefly. Dissolve the cornstarch in 2 tablespoons of water. Add it to the pan and cook until the sauce thickens. Stir in the sesame oil. Serve immediately.

Broccoli and Mushrooms

10 ounces Chinese broccoli, trimmed
6 ounces small mushrooms
3 tablespoons oil
2 cloves garlic, minced
¼ teaspoon salt
¼ teaspoon sugar
2 slices ginger, peeled, minced
1 tablespoon sherry or rice wine
Sauce:

> 2 tablespoons vegetarian oyster sauce
> 1 teaspoon cornstarch
> 1 tablespoon water
> ½ teaspoon sesame oil

1. Cut the trimmed brocoli into 2-inch lengths.

2. Mix the sauce ingredients in a bowl and set aside.

3. Heat 1 tablespoon of oil in a frying pan. Stir-fry the minced garlic. Add the broccoli and stir-fry briskly.

4. Sprinkle 1 tablespoon of water over the broccoli, cover the pan, and cook the broccoli for 1 to 2 minutes, keeping it crunchy. Add the salt and sugar. Remove and set aside.

5. Add 2 tablespoon of oil to the pan. When the oil sizzles, add the ginger and mushrooms. Stir-fry for 1 minute over high heat. Sprinkle 1 tablespoon of rice wine over the mixture.

6. Working quickly, return the broccoli to the pan and toss lightly. Push the vegetables to the side of the pan and add the sauce to the pan. Remove from heat as soon as the sauce thickens. Serve immediately.

$\mathcal{B}$est known by its Japanese name, daikon, the giant white radish is juicy, crunchy, and pungent. They are usually about 10 to 15 inches long, and about 2 inches thick.

Choose daikons that feel heavy and have a good white sheen. Avoid those that are spongy, brownish, and pithy.

Raw daikon marinated in a salty, vinegar dressing is commonly served at Japanese and Vietnamese meals. To tame its pungency, the Chinese prefer to pre-salt the daikon and let it exude some of its peppery juice. Used in stews, it turns surprisingly sweet and blends well with meats and vegetables. Grated daikon can be used as a filling for cakes and dumplings; mixed with ground rice, it is made into a steamed pudding that is indispensable in a Chinese New Year celebration.

Daikon
Giant White Radishes, Luobo

Daikon Turnovers

14 ounces daikon, peeled, grated
½ teaspoon salt
4 dried mushrooms
1 tablespoon oil
2 green onions, chopped
¼ carrot, peeled, grated
½ teaspoon sugar
½ teaspoon thin soy sauce
1 egg yolk, beaten
1 tablespoon sesame seeds
Pastry:
    2 cups all-purpose flour
    ¾ cup butter or shortening
    4 to 5 tablespoons cold water

1. Sprinkle the grated daikon with ½ teaspoon salt and let it sweat for 15 minutes. Drain. Squeeze out all the juice.

2. Soak the mushrooms in water until they are soft. Discard the stems and finely shred the caps.

3. Heat 1 tablespoon of oil in a frying pan. Add the mushrooms and the shredded daikon. Cook for 2 to 3 minutes. Remove from heat. Add the green onions, carrot, sugar, and soy sauce. Divide the cooled filling into 12 portions.

4. Preheat oven to 375°. Make the pastry by any dependable method. Divide it into 12 portions. Roll out each portion, making a 4-inch circle. Put a portion of the filling in the center, moisten the edges, and fold over to make a turnover. Glaze with the egg yolk and sprinkle with the sesame seeds.

5. Bake for 15 to 20 minutes until golden. Serve warm or at room temperature.

Daikon and Chile, Hunan-style

8 ounces daikon
1 teaspoon salt
2 mild red chiles, medium size
2 tablespoons oil
2 cloves garlic, minced
2 teaspoons vinegar
Salt and pepper, to taste
2 teaspoons cornstarch
1 tablespoon water

1. Peel the daikon and cut into fine julienne. Sprinkle with 1 teaspoon of salt and let the daikon sweat for 15 minutes. Rinse. Squeeze out as much juice as possible.

2. Remove the seeds and veins from the red chiles. Cut them into fine strips. You should have about ¾ cup.

3. Heat 2 tablespoons of oil in a frying pan. Add the minced garlic and the red chile strips. Stir-fry briskly over high heat.

4. Add the daikon and stir-fry for about 2 minutes. Do not overcook; it should remain crunchy.

5. Season with the vinegar and a pinch of salt and pepper. Push the vegetables to the side of the pan. Dissolve the cornstarch in 1 tablespoon of water. Add the mixture to the pan. Dish up as soon as the sauce thickens. Serve immediately.

Hot and Sour Soup

8 ounces daikon, peeled, shredded
1 small carrot, peeled, shredded
1 tablespoon oil
2 slices ginger
5 cups water
3 dried mushrooms, medium size
1 piece firm tofu, diced
1 ½ tablespoon vinegar
1 teaspoon salt
1 teaspoon soy sauce
2 teaspoons cornstarch
1 tablespoon water
1 egg, beaten
1 teaspoon sesame oil
¼ teaspoon white pepper
1 green onion, minced

1. Heat 1 tablespoon of oil in a non-metal pot. Add the daikon, ginger, and carrot. Fry them briefly. Add 5 cups of water. Simmer the soup, covered, for about 30 minutes.

2. Meanwhile, soak the mushrooms in water until they are soft. Drain. Finely shred the caps.

3. Remove and discard the ginger slices, daikon, and carrot . Add the mushrooms and tofu pieces to the pot.

4. Add the vinegar, salt, and soy sauce. Thicken the soup with the cornstarch dissolved in 1 tablespoon of water. Bring it to a boil.

5. Stirring the soup briskly, add the beaten egg. Add the sesame oil, white pepper, and green onion. Serve immediately.

*W*ith its thick, broad ribs curling around the main stalk, gai choy looks like a free-form sculpture. The crunchy ribs are the parts most commonly used; the leaves are tough and should be used only to flavor soups. Any stem that shows a white center is pithy, and should be discarded.

Gai choy's strong peppery bite is an acquired taste. Those who like it find its slight bitterness cooling and soothing to sore throats and hot tempers. The Chinese like to complement its strong taste with something equally strong, such as garlic and black beans, or to counteract the bitterness with a smooth, creamy sauce.

Pickled gai choy makes an excellent appetizer. Used in braised dishes, it loses some of its pungency and blends well with meats and vegetables.

Gai Choy
Broadleaf Mustard, Ogarashi
Mustard Cabbage

Pickled Gai Choy

8 ounces gai choy (4-5 stalks)
2 tablespoons vinegar
1 tablespoon sugar
¼ teaspoon salt
1 tablespoon oil

1. Trim off the root ends and tough leaves of the gai choy. Separate the large stalks from the central head. Clean and wash them thoroughly. Trim away the leafy portions. Slice the ribs diagonally into 1 x 2-inch pieces.

2. Heat a frying pan. Using no oil, toss the gai choy pieces lightly until they dry out and turn deep green. Do not overcook. Remove them and arrange in a serving dish.

3. Mix together the vinegar, sugar, and salt and let the gai choy marinate in the dressing at room temperature for 15 minutes or longer.

4. At serving time, drain off the liquid. Drizzle the gai choy with 1 table-spoon of oil. Serve cold or at room temperature.

Gai Choy in Coconut Sauce

1 pound gai choy
4 cups water
1 tablespoon oil
1 teaspoon salt
Sauce:
    2 tablespoons oil
    2 slices ginger, peeled
    1 clove garlic, pressed
    ½ cup whole milk
    ½ cup coconut milk
        Salt and white
        pepper, to taste
        2 teaspoons corn-
        starch
        1 tablespoon water

1. Trim off the root ends and tough leaves of the gai choy. Separate the large stalks from the central head. Wash the stalks thoroughly. Trim off the leafy portions. Cut the ribs into 1 x 2-inch pieces.

2. In a large pot, bring the water, oil, and salt to a boil. Add the gai choy and blanch briefly. Drain immediately.

3. Heat 2 tablespoons of oil in a frying pan. Add the ginger and garlic and fry them briefly to release their flavor. Discard the ginger and garlic.

4. Return the gai choy to the pan and turn the pieces gently in the oil.

5. Add the whole milk and coconut milk and heat gently. Season with salt and white pepper. Push the gai choy to the side of the pan. Thicken the sauce with 2 teaspoons cornstarch dissolved in 1 tablespoon of water. Serve immediately.

*G*arlic chives are closely related to the ordinary chives. They are milder in flavor, more fibrous in texture, and have slender, flat leaves. Chives are most abundant in late spring and early summer.

Garlic chives usually are sold in small bunches of 2 ounces each. Look for leaves that are young, tender and pale green. Leaves that are dark green and stiff are old. The white flower buds are delicious and decorative, but the flower stalks are tough. Occasionally, you can find pale gold chives that are grown in semi-darkness; these are very tender and expensive.

In Chinese cooking, garlic chives are used as a vegetable to complement bland ingredients such as tofu and eggs. Cut tender, young leaves into 1-inch lengths; older leaves should be finely chopped. Chives should be cooked quickly, in a little oil, to release their flavor. Overcooking makes them stringy.

Garlic Chives
Chinese chives, Jiucai

Fried Rice with Chives

3 cups cooked, long-grain white rice
3 tablespoons oil
2 eggs, beaten
1 slice ginger, peeled, minced
1 tablespoon water
½ cup minced garlic chives
Salt and white pepper, to taste

1. Use leftover rice that has been allowed to cool overnight. The grains should be firm and separated.

2. Heat 1 tablespoon of oil in a frying pan. Scramble the eggs over medium heat. Remove the eggs and set aside.

3. Reheat the pan and add 2 tablespoons of oil. Add the minced ginger and fry it to release its flavor.

4. Add the cooked rice, pressing gently with a spatula to separate the grains. When all the grains are coated with oil, sprinkle 1 tablespoon of water on the rice to soften it.

5. Add the minced chives and stir-fry for 1 minute. Return the eggs to the pan.

6. Season with salt and white pepper. Serve immediately.

Eggrolls with Chive

12 eggroll wrappers
Oil for deep-frying
Stuffing:

    3 dried mushrooms, medium size
    8 ounces bean sprouts
    2 eggs, beaten
    1 tablespoon oil
    3 ounces garlic chives, minced
    1 green onion, finely shredded
    1 slice ginger, peeled, minced
    ¼ teaspoon sugar
    Salt and pepper, to taste

1. Soak the mushrooms in water until they are soft. Discard the stems. Finely shred the caps.

2. Discard the discolored tails of the bean sprouts. Rinse and drain them well.

3. Heat ½ tablespoon of the oil in a small frying pan. Pour in half of the beaten eggs and cook on both sides to make a thin pancake. Remove from heat and set aside. Repeat this process for the rest of the eggs. Cut the egg pancakes into fine shreds.

4. In a bowl, mix together the ingredients for the stuffing.

5. Place 2 tablespoons of the stuffing in a corner of an eggroll wrapper. Roll it up diagonally halfway. Tuck in the left and right corners. Roll it up the rest of the way, moistening the remaining corner to fasten it.

6. Heat 1 inch of oil in a heavy frying pan to 350°. Deep-fry the eggrolls until golden. Remove and drain on paper towels. Serve immediately.

Stir-fried Chives with Tofu

6 ounces garlic chives
2 pieces tofu, firm variety
2 tablespoons oil
3 slices ginger, peeled, minced
1 teaspoon salt
½ teaspoon sugar

1. Rinse the chives. Cut into ½-inch lengths.

2. Dice the tofu into ½-inch pieces. Pat them dry with paper towel.

3. Heat 1 tablespoon of oil in a frying pan. Add the chives and stir-fry for 1 minute. Remove the chives and set aside.

4. Clean and reheat the pan. Add 1 tablespoon of oil. Add the ginger and stir-fry briefly.

5. Add the tofu pieces. Stir-fry over high heat for about 3 minutes.

6. Return the chives to the pan, add the salt and sugar, and correct the seasonings. Serve immediately.

Jicama is a root vegetable native to South America. It is shaped somewhat like a turnip and has a brownish skin. The meat is white, sweet, and crunchy.

Jicama is available practically all year round and is most abundant in the winter months. Although jicama can grow to a foot in diameter, most are between 4 and 6 inches around. Look for one with a smooth sheen to its skin. Because of its high water content, jicama spoils rather quickly. Store it loosely wrapped in a paper (not plastic) bag in the refrigerator.

Widely used as a salad ingredient in Mexican cooking, jicama endears itself to Chinese cooks because of its crisp texture and clean, sweet taste. It also is a handy and cheaper substitute for fresh water chestnut and lotus roots. Finely shredded, it can even be used like bean sprouts, and can stand up to cooking heat without going limp.

Jicama
Shage

Summer Salad

½ medium-size jicama
1 carrot
1 grapefruit
1 ounce thin rice noodles (maifun)
2 green onions, shredded
1 tablespoon sesame seeds, roasted
3 tablespoons peanuts, roasted, chopped
Oil for deep frying
Dressing:
    2 tablespoons vinegar
    2 tablespoons sugar
    2 teaspoons thin soy sauce
    1 teaspoon sesame oil
    2 slices ginger, peeled, minced

1. Peel the jicama and carrot. Cut into very fine julienne.

2. Cut away the peel of the grapefruit, including all the white membrane. Divide into sections and set aside.

3. In a frying pan, heat 2 inches of oil to 375°. Break the rice noodles into 2-inch lengths, and deep-fry them a small handful at a time. They should puff up at once into a crunchy, crinkly mass. Remove them with a strainer and drain on paper towels.

4. Mix together the ingredients for the dressing in a bowl.

5. The salad can be prepared ahead of time up to this point. Just before serving, toss the jicama, carrot, grapefruit, and green onions with the dressing. Top with the fried rice noodles, chopped peanuts, and sesame seeds. Mix lightly. Serve immediately.

Rainbow Medley

½ jicama (about 10 ounces)
1 cup diced bell peppers (mixture of red,
        green, and golden varieties)
1 to 2 jalapeño chiles (optional)
2 tablespoons oil
1 clove garlic, minced
1 teaspoon thin soy sauce
½ teaspoon vinegar
½ teaspoon sugar
Salt and white pepper, to taste

1. Peel the jicama and dice it into ¼-inch cubes.

2. Remove the veins and seeds from the bell peppers. Dice them into ¼-inch cubes.

3. If hot jalapeño chiles are used, remove their veins and seeds. Slice them thinly.

4. Heat a frying pan and add 2 tablespoons of oil. Over high heat, stir-fry the minced garlic, the jalapeño chiles (if used), and the bell peppers to release their flavors.

5. Add the diced jicama, soy sauce, vinegar, sugar, salt, and pepper. Toss lightly and dish up. Do not overcook. Serve hot or at room temperature.

S cabby and a botchy yellow-green in color, the kabocha squash is not pretty. Do not let its looks discourage you. It is surprisingly versatile and delicious. Easy to grow and highly nutritious, this native of South America is popular with Chinese farmers and has seen them through many famines.

Choose one that is dull-skinned and feels heavy for its size. Uncut squash can be stored in a cool, dry place for up to a month.

Despite its unattractive appearance, the skin is edible and should not be discarded. The meat is golden, mild, and firm. The fiber attached to the seeds tends to be gummy, and should be thoroughly cleaned. The scabs and blemishes on the skin should also be cut away.

Kabocha is similar to the acorn squash and can be baked or steamed and used in many American recipes. As a vegetable in Chinese cooking, it is usually braised, and the browning brings out its nutty flavor. Kabocha goes well with strong seasoning such as garlic and fermented black beans. Mashed, it can be used as a filling for cakes and puddings. The seeds can be roasted and eaten too.

Kabocha Squash

Rice and Squash, Country-style

¼ kabocha squash (about 8 ounces)
1 tablespoon oil
1 clove garlic, minced
1 slice ginger, peeled, minced
1 cup long-grain white rice
1 ¾ cup water
½ teaspoon salt
1 tablespoon chopped green onions

1. Clean the squash and cut off the ends and any scab on the skin. Do not peel. Scoop out the seeds and attaching fibers. Cut into ¼-inch cubes.

2. Heat 1 tablespoon of oil in a frying pan. Add the garlic and ginger. Add the cubes of squash. Fry them until they are golden. Remove from heat and set aside.

3. Put the rice, water and salt into a pot with a tight-fitting lid. Cover and bring to a boil. Turn the heat down to very low, and let the rice simmer until all of the water is absorbed, about 10 minutes.

4. Put the squash on top of the rice, cover the pan, and cook for about 10 minutes over very low heat.

5. Turn the heat off and let the rice steam for 10 to 15 minutes. Fluff the rice and squash gently with a fork and garnish with the chopped green onions. Serve warm or at room temperature.

Stir-fried Kabocha

¼ kabocha squash (about 12 ounces)
1 teaspoon salt
2 tablespoons oil
2 teaspoons sugar
2 tablespoons vinegar
Salt and pepper, to taste
3 slices ginger, peeled, minced
2 green onions, chopped

1. Clean the squash and cut off the ends and any scab on the skin. Do not peel. Scoop out the seeds and attaching fibers. Slice thinly into pieces about ¼-inch thick.

2. Put the squash pieces in a bowl, and sprinkle with 1 teaspoon of salt. Let the pieces sweat for 15 minutes.

3. Rinse the squash thoroughly. Drain and pat dry with paper towels.

5. Heat 2 tablespoons of oil in a frying pan. Add the squash and stir-fry for 6 to 8 minutes. The pieces should stay firm. Remove the squash to a serving dish and let it cool.

6. Dissolve 2 teaspoons of sugar in 2 tablespoons of vinegar. Season the squash with the vinegar mixture, salt, pepper, the minced ginger, and chopped green onions. Serve at room temperature.

Spicy Braised Squash

½ kabocha squash (about 1 pound)
2 tablespoons oil
5 cloves garlic, minced
2 tablespoons black bean sauce
1 cup water
Salt and pepper, to taste
1 tablespoon chopped coriander leaves
1 tablespoon chopped green onion

1. Clean the squash and cut off the ends and any scab on the skin. Remove the seeds and attaching fibers. Do not peel the squash. Dice it into 1-inch cubes.

2. Heat 2 tablespoons of oil in a frying pan. Add the squash pieces, and fry them until they are golden. Push them to the side of the pan.

3. Add the minced garlic, and then the black bean sauce. Stir-fry to release the flavor, about 1 minute.

4. Turn the squash pieces in the sauce. Add 1 cup of water, cover the pan, turn the heat down, and let the squash braise gently for about 15 minutes.

5. Season with salt and pepper. Sprinkle with the chopped coriander leaves and green onion. Serve immediately.

$\mathcal{T}$he barrel-shaped, compact napa cabbage has been available in supermarkets for a long time. Recently, the long, slender, green variety has become available as well.

Chinese cabbage is milder and more tender than the regular green cabbage, and can be used in similar ways. One of the most versatile vegetables used in Chinese cooking, this mild cabbage appears in many forms: it is eaten raw, dressed with oil and vinegar; it is minced and used as stuffing for dumplings; it is stir-fried, braised, and cooked in soups. It is even dried, salted, and pickled, and often is used to flavor other vegetables. In short, you cannot go wrong with Chinese cabbage.

Napa Cabbage
Chinese Cabbage
Celery Cabbage
Siew Choy

Cabbage Soup with Bean Threads

1 ounce bean threads (cellophane noodle)
2 tablespoons pickled turnip
8 ounces Chinese cabbage
      (about ½ head)
1 tablespoon oil
2 slices ginger, peeled
¼ teaspoon salt
2 cups water
2 tablespoons chopped green onion
½ teaspoon sesame oil
Salt and white pepper, to taste.

1. Soak the bean threads in cold water for 15 minutes. Drain. Cut into 2-inch lengths.

2. Finely shred the pickled turnip. Set aside.

3. Cut the Chinese cabbage crosswise into 1-inch pieces. Set aside.

4. Heat 1 tablespoon of oil in a pot. Add the ginger and then the cabbage. Stir-fry for 1 minute. Add the salt and the 2 cups of water. Cover and simmer for 15 minutes.

5. Add the drained bean threads and simmer for 5 minutes.

6. Pour into a soup tureen and sprinkle with the minced turnip, sesame oil, white pepper, and green onions. Serve immediately.

Spicy Cabbage Salad

12 ounces Chinese cabbage
1 tablespoon salt
1 cup water
1 fresh, mild red chile
2 small, dried hot chiles
1 tablespoon vinegar
1 tablespoon sugar
3 teaspoons oil
1 teaspoon sesame oil
3 slices fresh ginger, peeled, shredded

1. Halve the cabbage crosswise. And then cut it lengthwise into 3 x ½-inch pieces.

2. Dissolve the salt in 1 cup of water. Soak the cabbage for 30 minutes. Drain and squeeze it dry.

3. Discard the veins and seeds of the fresh and dried chiles. Finely shredthe fresh chile to make 1 tablespoonful.

4. In a small frying pan, heat the oil and sesame oil and brown the dried chile pieces. Add the shredded fresh chile and heat briefly to release their flavor. Pour the oil over the cabbage and toss briskly. Add the vinegar and sugar. Scatter the shredded ginger over the top.

6. Cover the dish, and let the cabbage sit for at least 30 minutes. Drain the excess liquid and discard the browned chile pieces before serving at room temperature.

*A*bout 8 to 10 inches long, with a smooth, shiny, purple skin and a green calyx, the Oriental eggplants are strikingly beautiful. They are milder than the round eggplants that are commonly found in the markets. In Chinese cooking, both varieties are used, but the long ones are preferred. Select a firm eggplant that feels heavy for its size.

To prepare the eggplant, pre-salt and pre-soak it to remove some of the bitter juice. This helps to prevent discoloration and reduce the amount of oil used in cooking. Eggplant can be deep-fried, braised, or steamed. Do not use cast-iron or aluminum utensils or the eggplant will take on the metal taste.

Eggplants are robust and strong tasting, and go well with strong seasonings such as garlic, chile, fermented black beans, and coriander leaves.

Oriental Eggplant
Japanese Eggplant, Chinese Eggplant

Stuffed Eggplant

2 eggplants (long variety)
2 tablespoons oil for frying
Stuffing:
    2 dried mushrooms
    2 tablespoons pine nuts
    3 pieces tofu, firm variety
    1 green onion, chopped
    2 teaspoons peanut butter
    1 teaspoon thin soy sauce
    ½ teaspoon sesame oil
    Salt and pepper, to taste

1. Discard the green calyx and end pieces of each eggplant. Cut each crosswise into 5 to 6 chunks. Soak them in salted water to cover for 15 minutes.

2. Meanwhile, soak the mushrooms in water until they are soft. Discard the stems. Mince the caps.

3. Roast the pine nuts in a dry frying pan. Chop them coarsely.

4. Mash the tofu, mix in the mushrooms, pine nuts, and the rest of the stuffing ingredients.

5. In a glass or stainless steel pot, parboil the eggplant pieces in water to cover for 5 minutes. Drain, cool, and pat dry. With a small knife, hollow out the eggplant pieces. Stuff the shells with the prepared stuffing.

6. Preheat oven to 350 °

7. Heat 2 tablespoons of oil in a frying pan. Add the stuffed eggplant pieces; brown them on both sides. Remove them to a greased baking dish. Bake until the eggplants are tender, about 15 minutes. Serve warm.

Spicy Eggplants

2 eggplants (long variety)
1 teaspoon salt
3 tablespoons oil
1 to 2 small dried red chiles, seeds
        removed
3 cloves garlic, minced
2 teaspoons black bean garlic sauce
1 tablespoon chopped green onions

1. Discard the calyx and ends of each eggplant. Cut each eggplant cross-wise into two pieces.

2. In a glass or stainless steel pot, heat enough water to cover the egg-plants. Add 1 teaspoon salt. Poach the eggplants until they are tender, about 10 minutes.

3. Remove the eggplants to a serv-ing dish. Split them open lengthwise with a fork.

4. In a small frying pan, heat 3 tablespoons of oil. Add the dried chiles and fry them briefly. Add the minced garlic. Immediately remove the pan from heat; do not let the chiles and garlic burn.

5. Discard the garlic and chiles. Drizzle the oil on the eggplants. Spoon on the black bean sauce. Using the points of a fork, carefully press the oil and sauce into the eggplants.

6. Garnish with the chopped green onions. Serve warm or at room temperature.

Braised Eggplants

2 eggplants (long variety)
1 teaspoon salt
3 cups water
2 tablespoons oil
4 cloves garlic, minced
2 slices ginger, peeled, minced
1 tablespoon water
1 tablespoon thick soy sauce
1 teaspoon sugar
1 green onion, chopped
6 sprigs coriander, chopped

1. Discard the green calyx and end pieces of each eggplants. Cut each eggplant lengthwise into 6 pieces.

2. Dissolve 1 teaspoon of salt in 3 cups of water. Soak the eggplant pieces for 15 minutes. Drain and pat dry.

3. Heat 2 tablespoons of oil in a frying pan. Add the garlic and ginger. Stir-fry for 1 minute to release their flavor.

4. Add the eggplant pieces and fry until they are golden.

5. Add 1 tablespoon each of water and soy sauce. Lower the heat, and cook until the eggplants are soft, taking care to retain their shape.

6. Add the sugar, green onions, and coriander. Serve immediately.

*M*any varieties of green peppers are available in the average market, ranging from the mild bell peppers to the fiery serrano and piquin chiles. Native to South America, peppers were introduced to China in the sixteenth century. Many varieties were rapidly incorporated into the Chinese cuisine, especially in the regional cooking of Sichuan and Hunan.

Bell peppers (green, red, and golden) are used as vegetables and are stir-fried, braised, or stuffed. should be

Used as flavoring agents in Chinese cooking, hot chiles mature and red. The veins are always removed, and the chiles are thoroughly fried in hot oil to release their flavor.

Red hot chiles also are used in their dried forms. They can be used whole, crushed, or pulverized. They also should be fried before being added to other ingredients.

Peppers
Chiles, Bell Peppers, Lajiao

Noodle Salad

6 ounces linguine
4 small, fresh red chiles
1 tablespoon oil
2 cloves garlic, minced
1 teaspoon sesame oil
2 tablespoons black bean sauce
1 tablespoon vinegar
2 green onions, finely shredded
4 radishes, sliced
2 tablespoons coriander leaves, chopped
1 tablespoon sesame seeds, roasted
Salt and pepper, to taste
Chile oil:
    5 tablespoons oil
    1 tablespoon ground chile

1. To prepare the chile oil, put the ground chile in a metal or heat-proof bowl. Heat 5 tablespoons of oil to just below the smoking point. Pour over the ground chile. Let the oil cool.

2. Cook the noodles in a large pot of boiling, salted water until tender but still firm. Drain immediately. Rinse under cold running water. Drain again.

3. Toss the noodles with 2 tablespoons of the chile oil. Reserve the rest of the oil for other uses.

4. Remove the seeds and veins from the hot chiles. Cut into thin strips.

5. Heat 1 tablespoon of oil in a frying pan, and fry the minced garlic and chile strips briefly. Add them to the dressed noodles.

6. Toss the noodles again with sesame oil and the rest of the ingredients. Season with salt and pepper. Serve at room temperature.

Peppers and Pine Nuts

½ green bell pepper
½ red bell pepper
2 small, fresh hot chiles
8 ounces tofu (firm variety)
2 tablespoons oil
2 tablespoons pine nuts
2 cloves garlic, minced
1 green onion, chopped
Sauce:
    2 teaspoons soy sauce
    1 teaspoon sugar
    ½ teaspoon salt
    3 tablespoons water
    2 teaspoons cornstarch
    1 teaspoon sesame oil

1. Dice the green and red bell peppers and the tofu into ½-inch pieces. Discard the seeds and veins of the hot chiles and slice them diagonally.

2. Mix the ingredients for the sauce in a bowl.

3. Heat 1 tablespoon of oil in a frying pan. Toss the pine nuts in the oil until they turn golden. Remove and set aside.

4. Add 1 tablespoon of oil to the pan. Fry the minced garlic and hot chile slices to release their aroma. Add the bell peppers and tofu pieces. Stir-fry for 2 to 3 minutes.

5. Push the vegetables and tofu to the side of the pan, add the sauce, and cook until the mixture thickens. Mix in the vegetables and tofu.

6. Sprinkle the pine nuts and chopped green onion over the vegetables. Serve immediately.

Chiles and Potatoes, Country-style

3 potatoes
2 medium-size chiles (mild variety)
2 tablespoons oil
2 cloves garlic, minced
1 teaspoon vinegar
Salt and pepper, to taste

1. Peel the potatoes and cut into julienne. Soak in cold water to cover for 15 minutes.

2. Remove the seeds and veins from the chiles. Cut into very fine julienne.

3. Heat 2 tablespoons of oil in a frying pan. Over high heat, stir-fry the garlic and chiles to release their flavor.

4. Drain the potatoes and rinse them until the water runs clear. Drain and pat dry with paper towels. Add the potatoes to the frying pan, and stir-fry them briskly for about 5 minutes. Do not overcook; the potatoes should stay crunchy. Add the vinegar and season with salt and pepper. Serve immediately.